THE VICTORIANS

JOHN MALAM

WAYLAND

HISTORY STARTS HERE!
The Victorians

OTHER TITLES IN THE SERIES
The Ancient Egyptians • The Ancient Greeks
The Ancient Romans • The Aztecs • The Tudors

Produced for Wayland Publishers Limited by
Roger Coote Publishing
Gissing's Farm
Fressingfield
Suffolk IP21 5SH
England

Designer: Victoria Webb
Editor: Alex Edmonds
Illustrations: Michael Posen
Cover artwork: Kasia Posen

First published in 1999 by Wayland Publishers Limited
61 Western Road, Hove, East Sussex BN3 1JD

© Copyright 1999 Wayland Publishers Limited

British Library Cataloguing in Publication Data
Malam, John
 The Victorians. – (History starts here)
 1. Great Britain – History – Victoria, 1837–1901 –
Juvenile literature
 I. Title
 941'.081

ISBN 0 7502 2365 0

Printed and bound in Italy
by G. Canale & C.S.p.A., Turin

Front cover picture: a wealthy Victorian family
Title page picture: a young girl selling flowers at St. Martin in the
Fields, London

Picture acknowledgements:
 The Bridgeman Art Library: front cover, 5, 7, 11, 12, 15, 17, 19, 20, 23;
CM Dixon: 28; ET Archive: 1, 4, 8, 18, 24–5; Mary Evans Picture Library:
6, 9, 10, 14, 16, 21, 22, 27, 29.

All Wayland books encourage children to
read and help them improve their literacy.

 The contents page, page numbers,
headings and index help locate
specific pieces of information.

 The glossary reinforces alphabetic
knowledge and extends vocabulary.

 The further information section
suggests other books dealing with
the same subject.

Find Wayland on the Internet at http://www.wayland.co.uk

CONTENTS

QUEEN VICTORIA

Queen Victoria ruled Britain longer than any other king or queen. She ruled for 64 years, from 1837 until 1901. This period of time is called the Victorian age. People who lived then are called Victorians, after the Queen.

Victoria was only 19 years old when she was crowned Queen of Great Britain and Ireland.

During the Victorian age, the number of people living in Britain increased from about 27 million to 37 million.

The Victorian age was a time of many changes. The Victorians were the first people to use some of the things we know today, such as telephones. This book tells you what it was like to live in the Victorian age.

During the Victorian age, factories were busier than they had ever been. Machines, at first powered by steam and then by electricity, made goods to sell all over the world. Britain became the most important industrial nation. It was said that Britain was the workshop of the world.

Victorian factories, like this cotton mill, used the latest machines to make their goods.

An exhibition was held to show people the thousands of different things made in Britain. More than six million people visited it. Queen Victoria went 30 times. It was called the Great Exhibition.

The Great Exhibition was held inside a huge hall of iron and glass. People called it the 'Crystal Palace'.

LIVING IN TOWNS

At the beginning of the Victorian age most people lived in the countryside. Only three out of every ten people lived in towns. By the end of the Victorian age it was the other way around. People had left the country to live and work in towns, where they hoped they could earn more money.

People who could not look after themselves were sent to live in a workhouse.

LIFE IN THE WORKHOUSE

Poor people without a job were given a place to stay and work to do in the workhouse. But life was still hard. The rooms were cold and the food was not good. Sometimes the people who ran the workhouses were cruel. Many people preferred to beg on the streets rather than go there.

In the busy towns there were lots of small shops. This scene shows Oxford Street in London.

In towns, the poor lived in badly built, overcrowded houses. But people with money moved to better houses built in the suburbs, on the edges of towns.

LIVING IN THE COUNTRY

Most people in the countryside worked on the land. From the land came clay for making pots and bricks, stone for building, wood for furniture, and food to feed the growing population in the towns.

People who earned their living from the land worked from dawn until dusk. Large families lived in tiny cottages, and had little food to eat. It was a hard life.

Horses worked on farms, pulling ploughs and wagons.

These people are going to a countryside fair. Their clothes show that some of them are wealthy and some are poor.

The people who owned the land enjoyed the best things in life. They lived in big houses, dressed in fine clothes and ate well. Life was good for them.

THE RICH

Most of the land was owned by just a few rich people. They were called the upper class. Their money and land was kept in their families. It was passed on from one generation to the next.

This painting shows rich people riding horses, and beggars, at the bottom, dressed in rags. To the right are two middle-class men.

A new group of people, called the middle class, appeared in the Victorian age. These people saw themselves as neither rich nor poor.

Middle-class people had jobs such as bankers, lawyers and doctors. Some owned factories, mills and warehouses.

The homes of middle-class families and their servants were very comfortable.

THE POOR

The biggest group of people was the lower class. These people were the poorest of all. They had little or no money, lived in the worst houses and ate the cheapest food.

Even people in the lower class could be split into groups, depending on the job they did. For example, butchers and bakers were seen as more important than chimney sweeps and road menders. People with no skills, and those who did not work, were the lowest of the lower class.

Lower-class people lived in dirty houses, called slums, that had no running water.

This man was in the lower class because he worked as a chimney sweep.

THE VICTORIAN FAMILY

It was common to have eight or more children in a family. Rich families had servants, who worked as cooks, maids and gardeners. The father of the family was the head of the household. He expected good behaviour from his children, and obedience from his servants.

Ordinary families liked to copy the Royal Family. Queen Victoria and her husband, Prince Albert, had nine children.

Going to church was an important part of family life. Nearly 12,000 churches were built by the Victorians.

In the early years of the Victorian age, women from poor families worked in factories. Rich women spent their time making their homes comfortable. Slowly, women's lives changed. In the last years of the Victorian age many more women from wealthier families went to work, often as typists or nurses.

CHILDREN

At the start of the Victorian age, children from the poorest families did not go to school. Instead, they were sent out to work. Children from wealthier families did go to school. They learned reading, writing, arithmetic and scripture.

By the end of the Victorian age all children aged between 5 and 13 had to go to school. It was the law. For the first time, children everywhere were taught how to read and write.

PARENTS

Victorian parents were very strict with their children. They taught them that they should be 'seen and not heard'. Children learned to be polite to adults and to obey their wishes.

Until the law was changed, children could be sent to work in coal mines and factories.

Indoors, boys played with toy soldiers and girls played with dolls. Outdoors they had spinning tops, hoops and marbles.

19

RAILWAYS

Railways were a new type of transport in the first years of Queen Victoria's reign. Most people had never seen a train or been on one. By the time Victoria was old, there were railways all over the country.

Railways moved people and goods faster and further than ever before. Food from the country reached towns in hours, still fresh.

Trains burned coal to heat water. The hot water turned into steam, and this powered the train.

Victorian railways were built by gangs of navigators, or 'navvies'.

Rail travel was cheap, so people began to take trips to the seaside. Holiday towns, such as Blackpool, grew up along the coast.

SHIPS AND TRADE

Because Britain is an island, ships have always carried people and goods to and from there. In the Victorian age, Britain owned more ships than any other country. Every year, the ships carried millions of tonnes of cargo all around the world.

IMPORTS

In the Victorian age, more people worked in the manufacturing industry than in farming. This meant that Britain needed to import more food from abroad. Raw materials also had to be imported.

Goods came to Britain by sea from all parts of the world. They were unloaded on to the dock and taken to towns and cities in Britain.

The Victorians invented the steamship. Like trains, steamships were also powered by steam. Steamships took over from ships with sails. They didn't need wind to blow them through the water because they could move under their own power.

In the 1840s, the steamship *Great Britain* carried people from Britain to America and Australia.

EMPIRE AND WAR

Australia, Canada, India and much of Africa were ruled by Britain. They were part of the British Empire. Countries in the Empire provided Britain with exotic foods, and raw materials such as cotton and rubber. British factories made them into goods to sell. Britain was a leading nation because of her Empire.

In the war with Russia, one of the most famous nurses of all, Florence Nightingale, looked after wounded soldiers. She tried to improve conditions in the hospitals too.

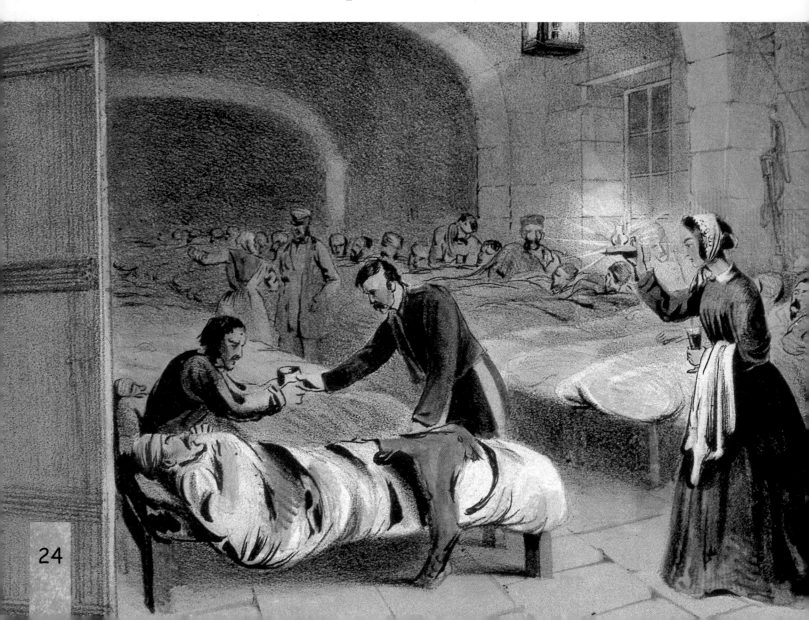

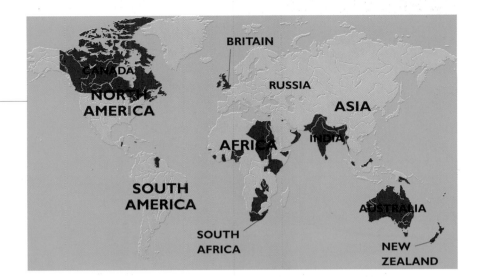

The areas shaded red were all part of the British Empire in 1900. As many as one quarter of all the people on Earth lived in the British Empire.

The Victorian age was mostly a peaceful time. But short wars were fought against Russia and South Africa.

INVENTION AND DISCOVERY

The Victorians lived in an exciting age. They saw the first bicycles, trams and motor cars on the roads. They were the first people to be photographed, and they saw the very first silent films on cinema screens.

The invention of the telephone, by Alexander Graham Bell, meant that people could talk to each other without being in the same room.

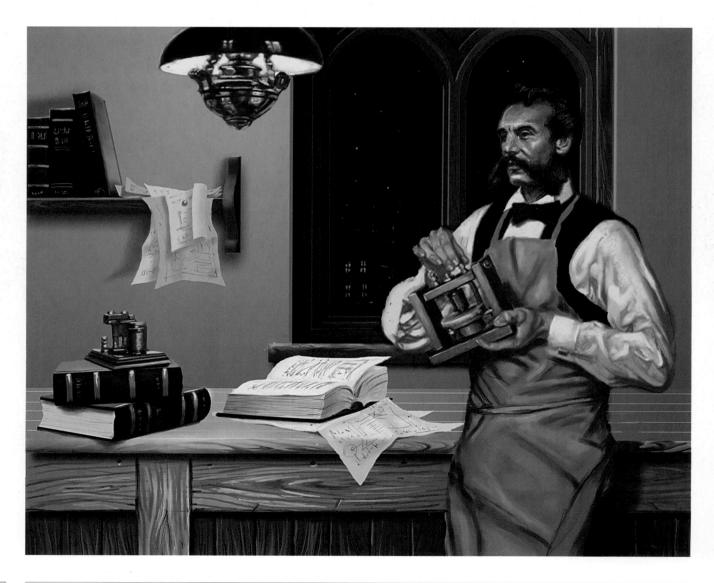

The motor car was invented in 1895. There were about 20 of them on the roads that year.

For the first time, electricity brought power and light into homes, offices and factories. In hospitals, chloroform was used to keep people asleep during operations, and germs were killed with antiseptics.

These and other inventions and discoveries changed the way that people lived for ever.

THE END OF AN AGE

The Victorians made many improvements which are with us to this day. Libraries, museums and art galleries were built. A police force was set up. Postage stamps were introduced, and Christmas cards, Christmas trees, and Valentine cards became popular. In sport, football, tennis and cricket took on their present-day look.

Child labour ended, working conditions got better and sewers were built – all of which led to better health for many people, especially the poor.

VICTORIA'S JUBILEE

In 1897 Britain celebrated Queen Victoria's diamond jubilee. She had been Queen for 60 years. The country celebrated with processions and parties.

The Victoria Memorial in London. It was built in 1911 to celebrate the long reign of Queen Victoria.

In 1901 Queen Victoria died. The nation mourned. The Victorian age had come to an end.

IMPORTANT DATES

1819 Princess Alexandrina Victoria was born.

1837 Queen Victoria came to the throne, aged 18.

1838 Queen Victoria was crowned, aged 19.
A gardener from Buckinghamshire became the first living person to be photographed.

1840 Queen Victoria married Prince Albert.
Postage stamps were first used, invented by Rowland Hill.

1840s The railways became very popular in Britain.

1842 Women and girls, and boys under 10, were banned from working in mines.

1843 Launch of the steamship *Great Britain*.
The first Christmas cards were sent.

1847 Chloroform was discovered by James Simpson.

1851 The Great Exhibition was held in London.

1852 The first free public library was opened, in Manchester.

1854–6 The Crimean War, in Russia.

1854 Florence Nightingale nursed wounded soldiers during the Crimean War.

1856 Every town had to have a police force.

1861 Prince Albert died from typhoid.

1864 Boys under 10 were banned from climbing inside chimneys to clean them.

1865 Antiseptics were discovered by Joseph Lister.

1868 The boneshaker bicycle was invented.

1870 Education was made available to every child.

1872 The first FA Cup Final took place.

1876 The telephone was invented by Alexander Graham Bell.

1878 Electricity was first used to light the streets, in London.

1887 Queen Victoria celebrated her Golden Jubilee, 50 years as queen.

1895 A motor-car factory opened in Birmingham, by Herbert Austin.

1896 Communication by radio waves was made possible, by Gugliemo Marconi.

1897 Queen Victoria celebrated her Diamond Jubilee, 60 years as queen.

1899–1902 The Boer War took place in South Africa.

1901 Queen Victoria died, aged 81.

GLOSSARY

British Empire Countries in all parts of the world that were ruled by Britain.

Child labour Using children to do work, such as working underground in mines, or in factories.

Chloroform A sweet-tasting clear liquid used by doctors to send people to sleep.

Class A group of people with many things in common.

Lower class The poorest people. They usually had the least money, lived in slums, did the dirtiest jobs, had poor health, and could not read or write.

Middle class This new class of people in the Victorian age ran businesses, owned factories, were well educated, and earned money for themselves through hard work.

Navvies Labourers who did heavy outdoor work, such as the men who built railways.

Raw materials Materials that are used to make something else, such as cotton which is used to make cloth.

Sewers Underground pipes and tunnels which cleaned up towns by carrying away waste matter and dirty water.

Slums The worst type of housing, usually in the centre of a town, which was lived in by the poorest people.

Steamship A ship that was powered by steam, and not by the wind.

Suburbs The edges of towns closest to the countryside, where good quality houses were built.

Upper class The richest people. They owned land, had a lot of money, and did not need to work for their living.

Workhouse A large building where people too poor to feed themselves lived.

FURTHER INFORMATION

BOOKS TO READ
The Victorians by Peter Hicks (Wayland, 1995)
Victorians by Ann Kramer (Dorling Kindersley, 1998)

Victorian Britain 1837–1901 by Andrew Langley (Hamlyn, 1994)
The Victorian Years by Margaret Sharman (Evans, 1995)

A Victorian Kitchen by Peter Chrisp (Heinemann, 1997)
A Victorian School by Peter Chrisp (Heinemann, 1997)

INDEX